Start TO finish
Second Series

FROM Egg TO Honeybee

LISA OWINGS

LERNER PUBLICATIONS Minneapolis

Lerner Publications Company
A division of Lerner Publishing Group, Inc.
241 First Avenue North
Minneapolis, MN 55401 USA

For reading levels and more information, look up this title at www.lernerbooks.com.

Library of Congress Cataloging-in-Publication Data

Names: Owings, Lisa, author.
Title: From egg to honeybee / Lisa Owings.
Other titles: Start to finish (Minneapolis, Minn.). Second series.
Description: Minneapolis : Lerner Publications, [2016] | Series: Start to Finish, Second Series | Audience: Ages 5-9. | Audience: K to grade 3. | Includes bibliographical references and index.
Identifiers: LCCN 2015036532| ISBN 9781512409086 (lb : alk. paper) | ISBN 9781512412970 (pb : alk. paper) | ISBN 9781512410815 (eb pdf)
Subjects: LCSH: Honeybee—Life cycles—Juvenile literature. | Honeybee—Juvenile literature.
Classification: LCC QL568.A6 O94 2016 | DDC 595.79/9—dc23
LC record available at http://lccn.loc.gov/2015036532

Manufactured in the United States of America
1 – CG – 7/15/16

TABLE OF Contents

Honeybees make honey. How do they grow?

First, the queen bee finds an empty cell.

A honeybee hive has three kinds of bees. Each hive has **worker bees**, **drones**, and a queen. Only the queen lays eggs. She moves through the busy hive until she spots a clean, empty cell.

She lays her egg in the honeycomb.

The queen dips her long body into the cell. She lays a single egg. The egg may or may not be **fertilized**. A fertilized egg will become a worker bee or new queen. An unfertilized egg will become a drone.

Soon the egg hatches.

The egg is long and white. It curls into the bottom of the cell. After three days, the egg hatches. Out comes a wriggling white **larva**.

Next, worker bees feed the larva.

The new larva is small. The worker bees feed
it a food called royal jelly. All larvae are fed
royal jelly at first. Most larvae later eat honey
and **pollen**. Queen larvae eat only royal jelly.

Worker bees cover the cell.

The larva grows plump. In about one week, it has finished eating. Worker bees cover the cell with wax.

Then the larva becomes a pupa.

In its cell, the larva spins a cocoon. It stays there for up to two weeks. During this time, it is called a pupa. Its pale body slowly changes shape.

The pupa slowly turns into an adult.

A head with eyes and antennae forms. The body sprouts legs and wings. The long, back part of the body is the last part to take shape. Then the pupa's eyes grow dark. Its body changes from white to gray.

Finally, the bee comes out of the cell.

The bee grows a light covering of hair. Then the adult bee springs to life. It eats its way out of its cell. It starts its life in the hive!

The new bees get to work!

The queen **mates** with drones to raise more bees. Worker bees make honey and gather pollen. We can thank honeybees for giving us honey and helping our gardens grow!

Glossary

drones: male bees whose only job is to mate with the queen

fertilized: made able to grow and develop. Fertilized honeybee eggs become female bees. Unfertilized eggs become drones.

honeycomb: a group of wax cells made by honeybees to store food and hold young bees

larva: the stage of an insect's growth between egg and pupa. When there is more than one larva, they are called larvae.

mates: joins together to produce young

pollen: fine yellow dust produced by plants

pupa: the stage of an insect's growth between larva and adult

queen bee: a female bee that lays eggs. There is usually only one queen in a hive.

worker bees: female bees that build, clean, and guard the hive. They also provide the food and raise the young.

Further Information

Glaser, Linda. *Not a Buzz to Be Found: Insects in Winter.* Minneapolis: Millbrook Press, 2012. Have you ever wondered what honeybees and other insects do in winter? Read this book to find out!

Markle, Sandra. *The Case of the Vanishing Honeybees: A Scientific Mystery.* Minneapolis: Millbrook Press, 2014. Check out this book to learn about bee colonies, threats to honeybees, and how you can help.

National Geographic Kids: Honeybee
http://kids.nationalgeographic.com/animals/honeybee
Check out this site for fun facts and photos about honeybees.

Nelson, Robin. *From Flower to Honey.* Minneapolis: Lerner Publications, 2012. Read this book to learn all about how honey is made.

San Diego Zoo Kids: Bee
http://kids.sandiegozoo.org/animals/insects/bee
Come to learn about bees and stay for more animal facts and games.

Index

Photo Acknowledgments

The images in this book are used with the permission of:
© Wildlife GmbH/Alamy, p. 1; © iStockphoto.com/GlobalP,
p. 3; © imageBROKER/Alamy, p. 5; © Donna Hayden/
Shutterstock.com, p. 7; Stephen Dalton/Minden Pictures/
Newscom, pp. 9, 17; © Scott Camazine/Alamy, p. 11;
© statephoto/Shutterstock.com, p. 13; © Jonathan Wilkins/
Science Source, p. 15; © iStockphoto.com/PaulJRobinson,
p. 19; © iStockphoto.com/alexadrumagurean, p. 21.

Front cover: © iStockphoto.com/proxyminder.

Main body text set in Arta Std Book 20/26.
Typeface provided by International Typeface Corp.

LERNER

SOURCE™

Expand learning beyond the printed book. Download free, complementary educational resources for this book from our website, www.lerneresource.com.